Love Your Naked Ass

Praise for
Love Your Naked Ass

"*Love Your Naked Ass* is a thought-provoking, paradigm-shifting guide that will inspire you to take the actions that will transform the way you think and feel about yourself and your life.

A must-read for any woman who is ready and willing to go after the self-love and pleasure she knows are her birthright."

~ Lisa Wilder, Intuitive Life Coach/Business Strategist
Founder of The Wilder Zone, www.TheWilderZone.com

"*Love Your Naked Ass* is a must-read for all women. I already feel better about myself after just one read through! I couldn't put it down once I started and now I'm excited to go back and work on the suggested exercises and take even more time to savor each chapter.

The best thing about this book is—it's fun, straightforward and simple. It doesn't overwhelm you with self-help type advice; but just uplifts your spirit with inspiring quotes (many by Kimberly herself) and simple actions you can take immediately.

I know I will be keeping this book handy to read from in my yoga classes and to my students. The book will serve as a reminder to myself to be confident, self-loving, develop a healthy body image, stay positive, have a good attitude, try not to be such a perfectionist and accept myself as I am.

Thank you Kimberly for sharing such a wonderful book and opening yourself up so freely to talk about your struggles and how you've learned to love your naked ass."

~ Kristin McGee, Celebrity Yoga & Pilates Instructor
Model, Spokesperson and Actress, www.KristinMcGee.com

"*Love Your Naked Ass* is boldly honest and speaks to that place we are all waiting to be spoken to about our bodies! Kimberly is brilliant in her 'no nonsense,' to the point attitude. The book is simple, and yet full of wisdom, powerful and uplifting messages of truth.

Every woman who has ever had a negative thought about herself ought to read this! As a society, if we can integrate the insights in this book, we would truly be better people with the power to create important change. It all starts inside."

~ Stasia Bliss, author of
The Chocolate Fast: Embracing Your Bliss One Truffle at a Time
and *Create Your Life (Not Just Babies)*

"When it comes to the "self help" genre, I like to read books that are straight to the point and that engage me instantly. Kimberly's book is exactly that, delivered with simplicity, empathetic warmth, and a no BS style, much like the author herself. The structure is refreshing—an inspiration, a quote and an action step—that's easily implemented in the moment.

Use this book as a powerful daily vitamin that will optimize and transform your physical and spiritual life. Go get yourself a lovely journal, your favorite pen, and open *Love Your Naked Ass* to any page— it's that friendly and that beautiful."

~ Laree D. Griffith, Producer and Social Media Manager
www.LareeGriffith.com

"*Love Your Naked Ass* is a thoughtful, inspiring go-to guide for women who are ready and willing to up their game. Whether you need to increase your self-esteem, soften your body hatred or let go of wanting to be a perfectionist, Kimberly can help. She is living proof that you can go from feeling lousy and worthless to feeling fabulous and on top of the world.

In this book, Kimberly delivers heartfelt, easy-to-implement steps that anyone can realistically do. These action steps can empower you to be the best version of yourself. A must-read for women of all ages."

~ Amber McCue, Life Change Strategist/Coach & Speaker
Founder of www.AmberMcCue.com & Co-Owner of Three Boudoir

Love Your Naked Ass

80 Gentle Ways to Transform Your Life,
Restore Your Serenity & Rediscover Happiness

Kimberly Riggins

Kimberly Riggins
Email: kimberly@kimberlyriggins.com
Website: www.KimberlyRiggins.com

Social Media
Facebook: www.Facebook.com/JoinKimberlyRiggins
Twitter: www.Twitter.com/KimberlyRiggins

Library of Congress Control Number: 2011960820

ISBN 978-0-98481-300-1

Warning—Disclaimer

The purpose of this book is to educate and entertain. The author and/or publisher do not guarantee that anyone following these techniques, suggestions, tips, ideas, or strategies will become successful. The author and/or publisher shall have neither liability nor responsibility to anyone with respect to any loss or damage caused, or alleged to be caused, directly or indirectly by the information contained in this book.

Dedication

This book is dedicated to my sister and best friend,

Jennifer Flipping.

Because of Jennifer, I have always aspired to be the best version of myself. After all, I am the big sister, she looks up to me, and I want to provide a positive role model she can be proud of.

I just hope I have lived up to the job. I love you.

Acknowledgments

I thank my parents for always giving me the space to find out who I was and what I was capable of. I appreciate and love both of you for always letting me find my own way.

To all of my friends, your support means more to me than I can ever express. Thank you for always standing behind me and rallying in my corner during the toughest of times.

To my cousin Cassandra, for creating a kick ass cover for this book. Your talent is amazing and I would never have been able to convey the image inside my head without you.

To Verna Wilder, my formatting fairy godmother. You have opened my eyes to a whole new world in print.

To Lisa Wilder, without your help this book would still just be words on some paper. Thank you for believing in me. Your friendship and coaching has been invaluable.

To my son Grayson, I never realized how much loving you would change me. You are a gift that keeps on giving and I love you with all my heart.

And to my husband Tony, without your love and support, I would not be the woman I am today. I will always love you.

Contents

My Story

I spent most of my life hating my body. Hell, hating myself. I was obsessed with food, with calories, with the number on the scale. I couldn't seem to get small enough. All I wanted to do was disappear.

And those damn mirrors...ugh, they were the enemy. Every time I looked into one of those damn things, I wanted to throw up. All I ever saw were my flaws.

To make matters worse, during this time, due to the lack of nutrients my body and brain were getting, I couldn't concentrate, which means I could barely function. I am sure waking up every morning, exercising six hours a day, living off of just two bagels and water didn't help.

The humor in all this is I thought I had everyone fooled. There was no way anyone knew how messed up I really was. On the surface, I appeared calm and collected. What a joke! I was a raving lunatic inside. I drank, slept, and ate "thinness" without considering sustenance.

Eventually I couldn't handle the pressure anymore. I hated everything about myself and knew that I needed serious help. So on February 14th; just a few weeks into my second semester of my freshman year of college, I took a medical leave of absence. I will never forget that dreaded phone call to let my parents know I was coming home.

The next few weeks, I went from studying literature, psychology and philosophy to sitting on the couch of a therapist's office to signing myself into a residential eating disorder clinic and then moving on to an outpatient therapy program. I spent the next few years working on myself, letting go of my eating disorder and trying to find balance.

My recovery process wasn't easy. It is really hard trying to eat 800 calories in one day when you were used to barely any at all. It was also mortifying that I had to admit that I was anything but "perfect."

There were certainly days I wanted to give up but I never did. I knew I couldn't go back. I knew I wanted to live a healthy life and I would do just about anything to make sure I beat the disorder. I have to say, by far, beating it was one of my greatest accomplishments.

I am no longer obsessed with food, nor do I hate the sight of my body. Sure, I may have a day or two when I don't feel "beautiful" but cut me a break—I am a woman after all. I now love to eat and I don't ever count calories.

This journey has truly been the best thing that has ever happened to me. I know that probably doesn't make much sense but because of my disorder I found my passion in life.

Every day I get to teach other women how to find balance with their eating. I get to help them see their true beauty and relinquish those inner voices. I have the pleasure of seeing them flourish in every possible way. It can't get much better than that.

The young girls and women I have worked with, I understand. They face every day the same self-esteem and body image issues that I did. I know what it is like to feel completely lost and alone and I believe I know what it takes to pull yourself out of that dark hole.

I am not a doctor, nor do I claim to be one, but what I do have to offer is firsthand experience and what worked for me. I decided to write this book, my first of hopefully many, for all of you who suffer from distorted illusions of themselves. And if we're honest with ourselves that's nearly all of us to one degree or another.

I want to bring you some inspiration through the power of words and give you some simple, gentle, action steps that can assist you in changing the way you see yourself. I want you to love yourself for who you are. It doesn't matter how tall or small you are, what you weigh, or what size clothes you wear.

It's about embracing all of who you are, inside and out, accepting it and relying on your inner power to propel you forward to greatness. I want you to be inspired to live life, not drown in it. And most of all, I want you to find the serenity and happiness that I found.

In this book, you will find quotes that inspired me to not only accept myself as I am, but that gave me the confidence and the self-esteem to heal. They allowed me to let go of my fears of not being enough, of wanting to be "perfect" and they served as a reminder that with positive thinking and the right attitude anything is possible.

Stop loathing yourself, stop making excuses and take the first step. The first step is always the hardest, but I promise it is also the greatest triumph the first time you put one foot in front of the other and move forward toward your goals and dreams.

I am here to help in any way I can. I am committed to your journey to self-discovery and self-love. I am living proof that it is possible.

So dig in, open the book to any page and take that first action step today. You won't be sorry and if you need help, I am only an email or a phone call away.

xo
Kimberly

How to Use This Book

On each page of this book, you will find an inspiring quote, some commentary, and an action step. Each action step has the power to initiate a change—in how you feel about yourself, how you handle a specific situation, or how you interact with others.

The quotes, comments, and action steps are not meant to cure you but rather inspire you in whatever way you need. You don't need to read the book in order. Choose a quote that speaks to you and follow through with the action step. The action steps may require you to do something or to write or to simply reflect.

The supplies you will need for this journey to make it most effective are easy to find: a journal and your favorite pen.

Just remember, taking any step, even a baby step, has the power to move you forward.

Enjoy the journey!

Body Image

Body image is how you see yourself and how you believe others perceive you. It is also how you feel in your body and about your body.

How you view your body can influence your psyche, your self-esteem, and your behavior. It can make you feel awful in your own skin, and it can directly affect your mood.

If you are constantly trying to remake or reshape your body, you may start to feel insecure and could lose confidence in yourself. This behavior affects every area of your life and especially your sexuality, your relationships, and your career.

When you consider yourself valuable

you will take care of yourself

in all ways that are necessary.

~ **M. Scott Peck**

Put Yourself First

I understand how difficult it is to put yourself first, especially if you have loved ones that count on you. It is so easy to push your wants and needs to the side while you are trying to take care of everyone and everything else.

But who really suffers here? You! When you put everyone else's needs and wants before your own, it is your health and well-being that is compromised.

Action Step:

Stop neglecting yourself. Set aside at least 10-15 minutes each and every day to do something that fills you up, provides you with energy, or makes you feel more like you.

Make this time a standing, non-negotiable appointment. Start small. Take a candlelit bath, play in your garden, meditate, take a walk, enjoy a yoga class, dance around the room, paint, draw, or stop and close your eyes and take a couple of deep, cleansing breaths.

It doesn't matter what you do with this time, as long as you use it to nurture yourself. The more you put yourself first, the more energy and stamina you will have to take care of everyone else.

Outside show is a poor substitute

for inner worth.

~ **Aesop**

Go Au Natural

I know how much pressure there is to look good and to fit in. The media (TV, internet, magazines) is constantly bombarding us with images of what "beauty" should look like, how we should dress, what makeup or product we should use, and what we should eat or drink to maintain their standards.

But the truth is, at the end of the day when your makeup is wiped away and your designer clothes are put back on the hangers, all you have left is…you.

Why not embrace yourself just as you are? Let your natural beauty shine through.

Action Step:

For one day, go natural. Forgo the makeup and wear clothes that you feel wonderful in. Choose garments that feel amazing against your skin, are comfortable and cozy but do not look frumpy. (Hint: no baggy sweatshirts or pants.)

Now go about your day, but for today, I want you to carry yourself as if you are the most beautiful creature on the planet, both inside and out. Because you are.

Before you retire for the night, grab your journal and reflect on how going natural made you feel.

Though we travel the world over to find the beautiful, we must carry it with us or we find it not.

~ **Ralph Waldo Emerson**

Stop Searching

We have all searched for the next promising product that will make us feel more beautiful...the new lipstick...the new designer jeans...the new face cream that is guaranteed to make wrinkles disappear. But if we can't look at ourselves "naked" and find beauty, none of the things we try will make us happy.

Products can't change who you are as a person. They may be able to enhance your appearance but they can never penetrate your inner beauty. Only you have the power to let that shine.

Action Step:

The next time you are getting ready to buy the latest, greatest beauty product, say no. Use your money on something else. Instead give yourself the greatest gift you could ever give yourself: self-love.

Perhaps you could luxuriate in a warm drawn bath, sipping a glass of wine, reading your favorite novel. Or maybe you could turn on some music and sway to the beat like no one is watching.

You could call a girlfriend you have wanted to chat with for months, go on a ME date and enjoy a nice quiet meal without any distractions or grab your favorite nail polish color, and after massaging your feet with lotion, paint your toes (or better yet, let someone else do that for you).

Everything has its beauty, but not everyone sees it.

~ **Confucius**

Learn to See Beauty

When you learn to see beauty in everything, you will also see beauty in yourself.

The little bird on your windowsill that wakes you up in the morning, the smell of fresh cut grass, the scent of freshly cut flowers, the roaring sound of the wind right before a storm...

Notice everything...take it all in.

Admire and cherish your surroundings. I promise if you can accomplish this, you will start to see yourself in a whole different light.

Action Step:

Grab your journal and write down three things that you find beautiful each day for the next 30 days. Make sure one of those three things includes something about you.

Your body is like a car . . . a vehicle to get from one place to another. The only difference is that you can always buy a new car, but you can't replace your body.

~ **Kimberly Riggins**

Take Good Care of Your Body

You only have one body, so you want to take good care of it. It is imperative that you strengthen yourself with proper nutrition and regular exercise. Your body is a sacred temple and you should treat it with the utmost respect, love and care. Without self-love, you are susceptible to obesity, eating disorders, disease or in severe cases, death.

I'm not saying this to scare you but to encourage you.

You need to take care of your body, inside and out. You would not put sticks, stones, and mud in your car's gas tank, so why would you feed your body Twinkies, soda, and donuts?

Action Step:

What is one step that you can take to show your body you care? Perhaps it is adding some fresh fruits and vegetables to your diet or blocking out 30 minutes a day to do something active. Whatever it is, don't delay...get started today.

When we lose twenty pounds . . . we may be losing the twenty best pounds we have! We may be losing the pounds that contain your genius, your humanity, your love and honesty.

~ **Woody Allen**

It's Never about the Number

I know that losing weight for some of you can dramatically improve your health (I have helped many do just that) but I also know that losing weight because you think it will bring you peace of mind, happiness, and contentment can have rather adverse effects on how you feel about yourself.

When you start fighting with the number on the scale, you tend to lose a sense of self. This can lead to depression, anxiety and feelings of inadequacy. You start hating yourself and forget to appreciate what is most important…that you are alive.

Action Step:

If you have an unhealthy obsession with your scale, don't stop to contemplate whether you should keep it or not, pick up the scale and throw it in the trash immediately.

Let go of the need to be a certain "number" and start being present to how you feel in your own skin. If you eat delicious, clean food, do you feel healthy? If you exercise and break a sweat, are you more energized? When you allow yourself a small amount of your favorite treat, do you experience pleasure? When you get enough sleep, do you wake feeling refreshed? Rather than focus all your effort on dropping your weight, why not focus on improving your overall health? Your weight will take care of itself.

Each individual woman's body
demands to be accepted on
its own terms.

~ **Gloria Steinem**

Celebrate Your Unique Form

You and your body are one of a kind. I know intuitively you already know that but I also know that there are times when you wish you could look like, or be, someone else. They may have the "figure" you want, the personality you desire, or the life that appears magical.

What you seem to forget is that you are not alone. Chances are the same people you wish you looked like, are wishing they looked like someone else, too.

Embrace your form. You were meant to be this person in this body here on Earth. Rather than trying to change her, why not show her off?

Action Step:

What is unique about your body? Do you have a birthmark that is unique to you? Do you have a hint of blue in your green eyes? Do you have strong, yet supple thighs? Small, yet perky breasts?

Grab your journal, and make a list of all the unique qualities about your body. Note all the things that would separate you from another. Turn to this page when you start wishing you looked like someone else.

I think that whatever size or shape body you have, it's important to embrace it and get down.

~ **Christina Aguilera**

Rock That Body

Your body is an amazing machine. Embrace it and show if off as much as possible. Take it out for a drive and show the world what it can do.

Instead of dwelling on the cellulite you have on the back of your thighs, try appreciating them for helping you walk across the room, run the marathon you signed up for, or for giving you the strength to pick your child up with ease.

Action Step:

Remind your body of how strong and powerful it is by putting it into motion. Have you been dying to sign up for that 5K? Fill out the registration form. Want to try out that new yoga class? Go. Interested in doing something a little risqué? Try pole dancing. Find a studio that gives lessons and schedule a private session.

It really doesn't matter what you do, as long as you just get your booty in motion today.

Realize that beauty is in every BODY and it doesn't matter what size or shape you are . . . it does not determine your worth or your character.

~ **Kimberly Riggins**

It's Not about the Size of Your Clothes

Whether you are a size 2 or a size 14, you are important and deserve to be loved. Your personality should speak volumes regardless of your size. Stop having negative thoughts about your appearance.

It is not serving you.

Avoid worrying about how you look to others as well…it enables you to feel powerless and gives you permission to play the victim. I promise you, this gets you nowhere.

If you let others determine how much self-esteem or self-worth you're entitled to have, you give up all the unique things that make you special.

Action Step:

If you are playing the victim in your own size war, STOP! If you are tormenting yourself with clothes that no longer fit you, donate them. If you feel ugly in everything you have in your closet, go treat yourself to a few new items that you think look fabulous on you. If you need some help realizing how fabulous you are, enlist the help of a friend.

Be true to yourself emotionally, physically, and spiritually without using your "weight" to define your life experiences.

~ **Kimberly Riggins**

Let Go of Your Dead Weight

Have you ever let the number on the scale dictate the quality of your day? Have you ever let a few extra pounds on your frame stop you from going out with your friends or from attending an event that could be a lot of fun?

Did you know that by letting your weight get in your way, you are essentially giving up your right to experience life?

I am going to ask you to stop this behavior today. I demand that you reach deep within yourself and find one thing you would like to accomplish but haven't because of your obsession with your weight.

Action Step:

If your weight wasn't a factor, what would you do today?

Would you ask that hot guy in your office on a date? Would you gather your girlfriends and get all dressed up to go dancing? Would you take a dip in the neighborhood pool? Would you allow yourself to be naked during the day in front of your boyfriend, husband, or partner?

Whatever it is, go do it! Right now!

Perfection

Trying to achieve perfection can often remind you of your weaknesses and shortcomings. It can cause unrealistic expectations and impossible ideals that you may feel you need to live up to. This may cause you stress, fear and anxiety and inhibit you from ever feeling complete or satisfied.

The thing that is really hard, and really amazing, is giving up on being perfect and beginning the work of becoming yourself.

~ **Anna Quindlen**

Accept Yourself as You Are

When you can embrace yourself with love and truly accept who you are, your whole life will shift.

You have amazing qualities that only you can offer the world. It would be a shame to hide them or hold them back because they are not "perfect."

What is one unique quality or gift about yourself you can offer to the world? How can you share that gift or talent with others?

Action Step:

Grab your journal and brainstorm all your gifts and wonderful talents. To jumpstart this process, ask yourself, "What are some things that I really enjoy doing? What are some things people compliment me on or say I make look easy?" If you start to struggle with this, ask a friend to help you.

Now take a look at this list and see what gifts and talents you are already using. If you have been ignoring most of them, find ways to apply some of those talents more fully into your life. Perhaps find a new hobby, volunteer, ask your boss for more responsibilities, or start a part-time business.

Life is too short to let your talents and gifts go to waste.

The artist who aims at perfection in everything achieves it in nothing.

~ **Eugene Delacroix**

Good Is Enough

It's not always about winning or having success in everything that you do. Many times, it is the effort put forth and the journey to get there that counts.

As long as you can, at the end of the day, say you did your best it doesn't matter if it failed or if it didn't work out. There is always tomorrow to try again.

Action Step:

Open your journal and write down three things you have always wanted to do or try but haven't because of the fear you might fail.

Now pick one and participate with abandon. Promise yourself you will not have any expectations about it and that you will not evaluate the results. Simply allow yourself to enjoy it.

People throw away what they could have by insisting on perfection, which they cannot have, and looking for it where they will never find it.

~ **Edith Schaeffer**

Open Your Blinds

If you are always waiting for a better version or what you think is the best version of whatever you desire, life will pass you by and you will never find true happiness. You will miss out on some extraordinary experiences. And the only thing you will be left with is regret.

Open your eyes to the possibilities. Walk through all the doors that are presented to you. Allow the mystery to unfold and be okay with the unknown. You never know what you might find…some of the greatest adventures of your life could be waiting.

Action Step:

Seize the moment. Take this opportunity to accept an invitation that you would normally decline. Go to that costume party, attend that sports game, or say yes to those dinner reservations.

If an opportunity is not presenting itself, don't sit back and wait, create your own experience. Spring for tickets to a live event, take an impromptu getaway, start a mastermind group of your own, or grab a friend and take tango lessons.

The point is to be unpredictable. Be daring. Be bold.

Art can never exist without naked
beauty displayed.

~ **William Blake**

Be Authentic

When you truly live an authentic life, you will be able to rid yourself of destructive habits, relationships and lifestyles. You will be able to find your inner strength and let go of all that plagues you.

You will be able to think for yourself and create your own thoughts, needs and desires. You will be able to take something so small and see the beauty that no one else notices.

Action Step:

Assess your authenticity. Take a timeout from your current life. This could be for a few minutes, a few hours or a few days (if you desire).

Pull out your journal, and reflect on what you are doing right now in your life that makes you happy and what you are doing that makes you unhappy.

If you need some gentle prodding, think back to when you were a child. What was it you wanted to do with your life? Does any part of your life resemble that today? What could you do today that could infuse your life with those desires?

Nobody can be perfect unless he admits his faults, but if he has faults how can he be perfect?

~ **Dr. Laurence J. Peter**

Embrace Your Flaws

Having flaws or faults makes you human. It makes you "real." It makes you unique.

What if you looked at your flaws as oysters that have not yet produced pearls? Everyone needs to sift through some sand to appreciate beauty.

Action Step:

Take out your journal, open to a clean page and list all of your so-called flaws. Next to each one, list how it can be viewed in a more positive, accepting way.

For example, instead of condemning yourself for being too stubborn, think of "stubborn" as being "strong-willed and determined." If you feel you are too blunt, why not look at this quality as being "honest and self-expressive."

Physically, if you believe your derriere is too large, why not kindly look at it as "curvy and sexy." If your abdominals look flabby, why not consider them "soft and sensual?"

Notice how much better you feel when you learn to find ways to love and appreciate everything about yourself.

It is reasonable to have perfection in our eye that we may always advance toward it, though we know it can never be reached.

~ **Samuel Johnson**

Have Realistic Expectations

It is so important to always put your best foot forward so you will have no regrets. There is nothing wrong with striving to be the best as long as you realize *your* best is good enough.

The key is to have realistic expectations. If you set your expectations too high, unattainable for anyone to reach them, you are setting yourself up to crash and burn.

Action Step:

Choose one of your current goals and rather than create a long list of what you think should happen, try not to expect anything…at least at first. I want you to instead focus on just being in the moment, giving it your best and neutrally observing what happens.

If your goal is to lose 10 pounds, rather than give yourself the unrealistic expectation of dropping those pounds in a week or two, why not focus on how good your body is feeling while eating wholesome, healthy food or how breaking a sweat leaves you feeling refreshed, energized and alive.

Switching your thoughts to what is going well while trying to achieve your goal is more effective than dwelling on what hasn't happened yet. Not to mention, it is easier to reach your goal when you are fueled with positive reinforcement.

Sometimes . . . when you hold out for

everything, you walk away

with nothing.

~ From the TV show Ally McBeal

Stop Stalling

Life is short. Moments are fleeting. And if you are constantly waiting for something else to come along to make you happy, feel more successful, or somehow complete you, you will always end up disappointed.

Life is not supposed to be "perfect." You will have ebbs and flows. Rather than hide from them, learn to challenge the ebbs and ride the flows. But no matter what you do, never stay stationary.

Stalling is an excuse you give yourself when you are afraid. Let your guard down and accept that things might not be exactly as you hoped they would. Who knows? They may be even better than expected.

Action Step:

Say no to your fears. Tell yourself that everything that happens today is a blessing and is supposed to happen exactly the way it does.

Before you go to sleep tonight, write down the events of your day in your journal and reflect on all the good things that came of it. No matter how small they may seem.

No one is perfect . . . that's why
pencils have erasers.

~ Unknown

You Are Allowed to Mess Up

Everyone makes mistakes. Both you and I have made decisions that at the time we thought were "right," later to find out we probably should have acted or chosen differently. The mistake isn't necessarily in the making or doing of something "wrong," but rather our attitude toward it.

Mistakes can actually serve as an opportunity to get to know yourself better. They can help us make better choices the next time around. And often they can be blessings in disguise.

Making mistakes is essential to your personal growth.

Action Step:

Change the way you think about your mistakes. Grab your journal, and describe one specific mistake you recently think you made.

How did you feel about yourself? What consequences did you receive or impose on yourself? What did you learn from making this mistake? What blessing did this mistake possibly offer you?

Even the best needles are not sharp

at both ends.

~ **Chinese Proverb**

Be the Best You Can Be

There are always going to be days when you feel "off." Days when you feel like you are unable to do anything right.

The key is to remember you don't always have to be perfect. Perfect doesn't exist. Just the simple fact that you tried is, and will always be, good enough.

Action Step:

The next time the perfection bug bites you, grab your journal and draw a "T" on the page. On the left side, make a list of all the benefits there are to being a perfectionist. One example of being a perfectionist is you always, regardless of what is going on in your life; have to have the house neat and clean.

On the right side, jot down the pain and dysfunction that is associated with each benefit. In this case, trying to always keep the house neat and clean takes away valuable time you could be spending with your family and friends.

This exercise will help you see the absurdity of trying to be perfect. The pain and dysfunction will always far outweigh the benefits.

To me, perfection is the beauty
in imperfections.

~ **Kimberly Riggins**

Be a Diamond in the Rough

Every woman on the planet encompasses beauty. That includes you. You have something so unique that no one else in the world has.

Give yourself permission to practice being imperfect. It creates your character. It gives you strength and it oozes juicy, natural goodness.

Action Step:

Practice being imperfect. Find something you do "perfectly" and mess it up.

If you are always on time and even early, show up two minutes late. If you always perfectly match, wear mismatched socks or undergarments. If you rewrite your notes because you think they are sloppy, write sloppy on purpose.

Have fun with this. Messing up little things deliberately can help you realize striving for perfection is so overrated.

Self-Esteem

Self-esteem is how much you value yourself and how important you think you are. It's how you see yourself and how you feel about your accomplishments.

Self-esteem isn't about bragging about how great you are. It is about knowing that you're worth a lot. It's not about thinking you're perfect but knowing that you're worthy of being loved and accepted.

To forgive is to set a prisoner free

and discover that the prisoner

was you.

~ **Lewis B. Smedes**

Learn to Forgive

Have you ever made a mistake or a decision that you could not take back? I know I have but dwelling on it is not the answer. The reality is whatever happened is in the past, the only thing we have control over today is the present.

You have the power to determine what you hold on to and what you let go of. If you have made a mistake that has caused you to feel less worthy, then you need to forgive yourself.

Think of forgiveness as another act of love. You would forgive someone else you love, so why not start with yourself?

Action Step:

What is one thing you know you need to forgive yourself for?

When I have trouble forgiving myself, there are three things that I do to help me let go of the past. I create a mantra, journal and perform a random act of kindness. Creating a mantra and repeating it over and over again helps me change my thought patterns. Journaling allows me to reflect on my feelings without allowing them to fester in my body and performing a random act of kindness refills my worth quotient and reminds me why I am here, to help others.

Which one of these three things will you try today?

He who trims himself to suit everyone

will soon whittle himself away.

~ **Raymond Hull**

Do Not Compromise Your Values

Everyone has a set of values they live by. Unfortunately, when you are trying to make someone else happy by being someone you're not, your values become blurred, almost unrecognizable.

If you continue down this path of conforming yourself to meet another's needs, you will never be happy and never experience inner peace.

You have to make up your own set of rules. Be clear on your values and live in harmony with them.

Action Step:

The first step is to identify what your values are. Grab your journal and write down your most precious values in life. Circle your top three. Are they love, connection to family and passion? Or are they happiness, security and adventure?

Ask yourself if you have been living in line with your values or if you have been conforming to someone else's.

Regardless of where you are, make a commitment to yourself today to make a small change in your life that will keep your values in sync.

Low self-esteem is like driving through life with your hand-break on.

~ **Maxwell Maltz**

Open Up the Road

Life is full of surprises, twists and turns and experiences that you deserve to take part in. Do not limit yourself out of fear of the unknown.

Face the fear head-on and do it anyway. Put your foot on the gas and go! Your destination is waiting.

Action Step:

Open your journal to a clean page and write "My Fears" at the top. Now take 5-10 minutes and write down every fear that pops into your head.

Now divide them into two categories, personal and professional. Review your list and next to each fear, write down one action step that would help you overcome that fear.

For example, I used to have a fear of public speaking, so one action step I took to overcome that fear was I signed up to speak at a small conference. The size of my class was approximately 15-20 people. It was just the right size to get my feet wet and to learn to get comfortable speaking in front of others.

What small step are you going to take to overcome one of your fears?

Listen to your heart above all
other voices.

~ **Marta Kagan**

Your Heart Is Always Right

Your mind likes to battle. It likes to make you doubt your feelings, your wants, and desires.

You have a choice. You can listen to your mind and always feel let down or regret the decision that you made, or you can follow your heart.

Your heart will always guide you to the right place. Trust in yourself. Your heart will never steer you wrong.

Action Step:

When faced with your next major decision, whether or not to stay in a relationship, take that new job you were offered, or move to a different state, I want you to perform this simple, yet enlightening breathing exercise.

Find a quiet space, sit down and close your eyes. As you take a deep breath in, and a deep breath out, ask yourself, "What is it I really want?"

Pay close attention to what you body is telling you. Continue asking this question until your whole being is vibrating with the right answer. You will know it when you feel it.

Never bend your head. Always hold it
high. Look the world straight
in the face.

~ **Helen Keller**

Never Be Afraid to Be Yourself

There will be people in your life who want to see you fall. They may even try to knock you down. But you have the strength to hold your ground.

Stand tall in your convictions. Be proud of who you are. And show those people and the world that you are not afraid of them. Nor are you afraid to be yourself.

Action Step:

To raise your self-esteem instantly, I want you to practice walking with your head held high today. Stand tall. Keep your shoulders back. And whatever you do, no slouching!

Every time you cross someone else's path, I want you to make eye contact. And last but not least, smile!

Someone's opinion of you does not
have to become your reality.

~ Les Brown

You Hold the Power

It is a sad but true fact that most people care what others think of them. It can shape who you are if you believe what they say. But what do they really know about you?

Their opinions have no value if you don't allow them to. You get to show people what you want them to see and if they are blind to your brilliance, they were not meant to be in your life.

Action Step:

Today, I want you to practice listening with open ears. I want you to really hear what people are saying about you and the rest of the world.

Remind yourself that what others say about you is merely their opinion. The only opinion that counts in regard to you is your own.

Take note of the people and words that impact you the most. If you hear something negative, what can you do to lessen the blow? Reflect your thoughts in your journal.

Every individual has a place to fill in
the world and is important in some
respect whether he chooses
to be so or not.

~ **Nathaniel Hawthorne**

Accept the Challenge

I believe you were put on this planet with a purpose. You may not know what your purpose is yet, but it's there. Perhaps the best advice I ever got was to be patient, and trust that your purpose will come when you are ready to receive it.

Until then, accept the challenge the Universe has bestowed upon you. Experiment with everything that brings you any sense of joy. Your purpose will come and when it does…you will know it.

Action Step:

Stop forcing yourself to figure everything out right now. Just enjoy being present.

Today, I want you to focus on the here and now. Use all your senses. Look at what is right in front of you. Feel the objects you come in contact with. Listen to the sounds around you. Smell your environment.

Before retiring for the evening, describe your experience. Did it turn from an ordinary day to an extraordinary one?

Let the world know you as you are,
not as you think you should be,
because sooner or later, if you are
posing, you will forget the past, and
then where are you?

~ **Fanny Brice**

Practice Being You

Trying to be someone you are not takes a lot of energy and a whole lot of effort. Eventually you will forget and the real you will surface.

Why not just skip the nonsense and be true to yourself? Show up every day as YOU!

Action Step:

Today, forget how you think you "should be" and focus on who you really are and what it is you really want. Pay attention to how you feel, what you're thinking, what you say and how you show up.

Give everyone you come into contact with definitive answers today. Do not use "I don't know," or "I don't care." Because the truth is, you do care and you do know exactly what you want.

Reflect your experience in your journal. How did it feel to be authentically you today?

If you want a quality, act as if you already had it.

~ **William James**

Fake It Until You Make It

While working with clients, I often request that they keep a "Be Journal." It is a running list of traits or adjectives that describe how they want "to be."

You were born with a specific set of traits or qualities. There may be some qualities you do not have that you admire. Those traits can be learned.

Action Step:

Create a list in your journal of all the traits you would love to possess.

Would you like to be persuasive, tenacious, patient, practical, confident, thoughtful? Come up with at least 5-10 traits. Now circle the one you wish you had the most.

What would happen if you acted "as if" you already had that trait? How would you act? What would you do? What kind of body language would you have? How would others respond to you?

To make this trait your own, you have to try it on and experience how it feels. Eventually with practice, you will own it.

You have within you right now, everything you need to deal with whatever the world can throw at you.

~ **Brian Tracy**

You Have Amazing Strength

I truly believe the Universe gives you only what you can handle. If your life is going through a rough patch right now, it will be okay. You will get through it. And you will be stronger on the other side.

You may not see it now but a year from now, five years from now, you will look back on that moment and see not only the lesson you were supposed to learn but the triumph of having overcome that hurdle or situation.

Action Step:

It's time for you to get honest with yourself. Take out your journal and ask yourself, "What struggle am I faced with right now? What lesson am I supposed to learn from this? What is one small step I can take to help myself climb over this hurdle or to fix this situation?"

If you are having relationship issues right now, rather than blame your partner, spouse, friend or coworker you are in the relationship with, ask yourself what you could do to improve the situation. Is it to be a better listener, to be more cooperative, to be more loving?

Find one small thing you can do to shift this situation today.

Confidence

Self-confidence is the difference between feeling afraid and feeling unstoppable. Your perception of yourself impacts how others perceive you. Perception is reality—the more self-confidence you have, the more likely it is you'll succeed.

Whether you think that you can, or that you can't, you are usually right.

~ **Henry Ford**

Put Trust in Your Abilities

Have confidence in your abilities and know that if you approach it with your heart and soul, you can accomplish anything. If you are having trouble with this area of your life, visualize the end result and work backwards, envisioning the steps you took to get there.

Your thoughts are very powerful…you are the only one who can stop yourself from accomplishing your goals. Always give yourself the benefit of the doubt.

Action Step:

Give up thinking you can't. Delete "can't" from your vocabulary. When faced with a situation where an action is needed, ask yourself, "How can I make this happen?"

Keep a running list of when you use "can't" in your journal. Take notice if there are any connections. Take the time to rephrase your statement using the words, "I can."

If you hear a voice within you say 'you cannot paint,' then by all means paint, and that voice will be silenced.

~ **Vincent Van Gogh**

Just Do It

Have you ever had a little voice inside your head tell you that you are not good enough because you are too stupid or make too many mistakes, or that you don't have what it takes to accomplish your goal, that you have no real talent?

This is something I have definitely faced head-on numerous times in my life. This is also something that comes up at some point in every session I have ever had with a client. I know firsthand what it feels like to think you are not good enough, smart enough, pretty enough. It's sad really. Why do we insist on getting in our own way?

The solution is simple: as Nike would say "Just Do It!" Action solves paralysis and quiets those voices for good.

Action Step:

What are three things you have wanted to do for the longest time but let your "voices" talk you out of? Write those three things down in your journal and next to each one, write down all the excuses you have made for not doing them. Are any of your excuses valid?

If you have wanted to learn how to salsa dance but keep making the excuses that you don't have the time, or you will look silly because you don't know how to dance, don't fret. Do it anyway. Schedule the lesson and go. You will never know how much fun you could have had unless you try it.

Feeling successful is a state of mind.

~ **Kimberly Riggins**

Create Your Own Reality

You have complete control over what happens to your life. And you determine what defines your success. No one else has the ability to take that success away from you unless you let them change your mind on how your success is measured.

Feeling successful is really a state of mind. When you feel successful, you act successful and when you act successful, you take consistent action.

Action Step:

List 10 of your top achievements.

Write them down somewhere you can see them often. Perhaps keep a running list in your journal and your top 10 on a sheet of paper. Hang your top 10 in a place you look at often, such as the mirror in your bathroom, your bulletin board in your office, or on the back of your bedroom door.

Whenever you begin to question your success, come back to your list and review all you have accomplished.

If my mind can conceive it, and my
heart can believe it, I know
I can achieve it.

~ **Jesse Jackson**

Have Faith

You are a powerful, intelligent, amazing being who can accomplish anything you put your mind and heart into. Always have trust and faith in yourself to make the right decision.

Believe in the possibility that there is a force in the Universe that is bigger than you and if you are clear about what you want, the Universe will provide.

Action Step:

Today, you are going to practice having faith in yourself.

Before you leave your house, visualize how your day is going to turn out. Picture yourself succeeding at whatever it is you have to accomplish. Our mind thinks in pictures so feed it images. If you find yourself getting stuck, take a moment to regroup.

Take 3-5 deep breaths and remind yourself that whatever challenge may arise today, it will work itself out. Tell yourself that you have everything you need in life to face this challenge head on and that the Universe has your back.

Don't live down to expectations. Go out there and do something remarkable.

~ **Wendy Wasserstein**

Strive for More

There will be people in your life that don't believe in you. People who want to see you fail. Do not take it personally. It really is not about you. It is about them and their lack of confidence and self-esteem.

Never conform yourself to meet their expectations because if you do, you will find yourself unhappy and unfulfilled.

Follow your passion even if everyone else questions it. You were put on this Earth to do something remarkable. Only you can determine what that is. Do not hold yourself back. Keep pushing yourself forward and always strive for more.

Action Step:

What is your passion? Are you in love with art? Finance? Writing? Helping those in need?

Take 10 minutes today and journal about your passion. What is it that lights you up? Makes you smile from ear to ear?

Are you currently doing that? If not, how can you find time in your schedule to add some of these activities?

I am not a has-been. I am a will be.

~ **Lauren Bacall**

A Steady Pace Wins the Race

Everyone moves at different speeds. Some people peak much younger than others but that doesn't make you less of a person if you are not exactly where they are...in life, in love or in your career.

When the time is right, you will shine. It is not always important who gets out of the gate the fastest, it is the one who can last the longest that counts.

Action Step:

Take some time to reflect on what is truly your pace in life. Do you move quickly or are you happier moving at a slower speed? Are you honoring that pace? If not, slow down or speed up.

Go out in the world and work like money doesn't matter. Sing as if no one is listening. Love as if you have never been hurt, and dance as if no one is watching.

~ **Unknown**

Learn to Let Go

Pure confidence comes when you can act crazy and have fun and not care what other people may think. It is when you can take consistent action in every area of your life without having any expectations from another. It is about letting go of other people's random perceptions and being true to yourself.

Live your life with utter abandon. Open yourself up to the world. Allow yourself access to every possibility. Here you will find true happiness.

Action Step:

What is one crazy thing that you could do today? Have you always dreamed of dancing in the rain? Skinny dipping in the ocean? Eating chocolate naked?

Regardless of what it is, make sure it is something that you know would fill your spirit, challenge your mind and warm your soul. Now pick one and do it with reckless abandon.

Too many people overvalue what they
are not and undervalue what
they are.

~ **Malcolm S. Forbes**

Accept Your Greatness

You have so much to offer the world. Everyone, including you, has something to contribute. It is so important to never underestimate your value.

Let go of the things you cannot change and put forth your greatest attributes instead. Lead with your greatest strengths in everyday encounters, and watch your life unfold in a whole new way.

Action Step:

What are five of your best strengths?

Are you extra loving, nurturing, funny, a great conversationalist, sensitive, a wonderful listener, kind to others, or generous? Open your journal and list them.

Do you use these strengths every day? Is there a way you can incorporate them in everything you do?

If you find yourself having trouble with this exercise, ask a friend for help. Someone who knows you well will be able to help you pinpoint your strengths and often they will be able to see things you are unable to.

A man can stand a lot as long as he can stand himself. He can live without hope, without friends, without books, even without music, as long as he can listen to his own thoughts.

~ Axel Munthe

No More Inner Critic

If you can learn to fight and ignore your inner critic, you can handle anything life hands you. Remember, you are always going to be tougher on yourself than anyone else could be.

It is imperative that you realize that those negative comments you hear in your head are just repetitive, unoriginal thoughts meant to mess with you.

If you choose to not listen, and you take the time to recognize when they occur, you will find yourself in a much more positive, loving space. It is in this place you can develop and refine your self-confidence.

Action Step:

Today, I want you to keep your journal near by. Each time you have a negative thought, I want you to write it down.

Later, I want you to review these thoughts. Do they all sound the same? Where or who do you think influenced these thoughts? Can you turn those negative thoughts into positive affirmations or statements instead?

Take each negative thought and change it into a positive affirmation or statement.

Be beautiful if you can, wise if you want to, but be respected—that is essential.

~ **Anna Gould**

Show Yourself Some Respect

In order to really respect others, you must first learn to respect yourself.

I have seen many women, as well as men, condemn themselves for who they are because of qualities they encompass that they don't like. We all have qualities or personality traits we are not happy with.

The key is to focus on the ones you do like and approach the ones you dislike with grace.

Action Step:

Look at your negative traits through different glasses...see if you can find something positive in them.

I hate that I speak before I think. I have gotten myself into a lot of hot water because of this trait; however, at times, it has also served me well. Typically in a brainstorming session or in a group setting, while everyone else is quiet because they fear they may look stupid, I am the first one to utter a word. This trait sometimes helps break the ice.

What is one of your negative traits you wish you could change? Can you see how this trait may potentially help you?

Love

When you can love yourself completely and wholeheartedly, you have the ability to be yourself. You feel nurtured, are able to take risks without feeling you will be rejected, and can show vulnerability, and be able to have open, and honest, relationships with yourself and others.

Plant your own garden and decorate your own soul, instead of waiting for someone to bring you flowers.

~ **Veronica A. Shoffstall**

Sing Your Own Love Song

Through my work with clients, I realized the stories are always the same. "No one loves me. I am not good enough. I will never be happy."

They wait impatiently for my response as though I will have the magic cure to their problem. They are all surprised with the huge wake up call they get instead.

You don't need someone in your life to make you feel worthy, important or loved. If you can't feel these things for yourself, I guarantee you will be searching for them for the rest of your life.

Action Step:

Grab your journal and create a love list. Commit to writing at least 50 things you love about yourself.

Start with the small things. You may think you have a great smile, beautiful eyes, able hands, or a great sense of humor. You may be a hard worker, a talented singer, dancer or writer.

The key is to keep adding things to this list...dare to create 100 things you love about yourself.

The way you treat yourself sets the
standard for others.

~ **Sonya Friedman**

Be Kind to Yourself

Have you ever been disappointed when someone else treats you badly or doesn't give you the respect you deserve? Did you ever stop to think it may be because of the way you treat yourself?

If you don't treat yourself with respect, love, and honor, how can you really expect anyone else to? Always treat others the way you would want to be treated. If they can't reciprocate, then they don't respect you and it is time you find new people to surround yourself with.

Action Step:

Today, regardless of who you are around, treat them the way you would want to be treated. Be kind, offer your help, give compliments, be honest with them, and show them affection.

Later, grab your journal and reflect on how this experience made you feel. If someone was not reciprocating your kindness, how did it feel for you to kill them with kindness anyway?

Monkeys are superior to men in this:
when a monkey looks into a mirror,
he sees a monkey.

~ **Malcolm De Chazal**

What You See Is What You Get

I was watching my son admire himself in the mirror the other day and it made me remember that when I was young, it took little effort to look at myself and smile. I didn't see any flaws, or imperfections. I didn't allow my insecurities to create images that were not really there.

I just loved what I saw. I couldn't take my eyes off myself. I was fascinated by everything...the way my forehead wrinkled when I laughed, the shape and color of my eyes, even the fact that I had huge lips (better to kiss with my mother used to say).

But somewhere along my journey, I became my worst critic...I couldn't find anything I liked about myself. Can you relate?

Action Step:

Today, I want you to stand in front of a mirror and look at yourself through a different lens. Can you look at your crow's feet as signs of how much your life made you laugh? Can you see your forehead lines as symbols of your expressive self?

What about those stretch marks that appeared after you gave birth or had a surgical procedure? Can you look at those lines as medals of strength?

Be kind and loving as you do this exercise...do not give your inner critic any thoughts to work with.

Self-love is often rather arrogant than blind; it does not hide our faults from ourselves, but persuades us that they escape the notice of others.

~ **Samuel Johnson**

You Are Okay Just the Way You Are

I used to believe that everyone could see my flaws. That when others' looked at me, my imperfections were front and center. What I didn't realize is that those beliefs were just another game my mind played on me.

The fact is I have flaws...you have flaws...everyone does.

The key is to learn how to be okay just the way you are. The most effective way to do that is to practice unconditional love, both toward yourself and others.

Action Step:

Show yourself some appreciation today. What could you give yourself or do for yourself that would give your body, mind and soul the appreciation it deserves?

Perhaps a day off to play, a trip to the beach to relax, a quick manicure and some lunch, popcorn and a movie, or a walk or hike in the park.

If you are having trouble coming up with ways to appreciate yourself, think about how you appreciate others. What do you do for them? Could you see doing something similar for yourself?

Self-love is the greatest of all flatterers.

~ **Francois de la Rochefoucauld**

Compliment Yourself

Receiving a compliment from someone else is always special but if you don't believe what they have said, it means nothing.

If you can look at yourself and find something to admire, you are halfway there. If you can't, don't give up trying. I never thought I would be able to look at myself and like what I saw but I can.

It starts with a small step…what compliment can you give yourself today?

Action Step:

Every morning upon waking and before you leave your bedroom, look into the mirror and give yourself a compliment.

Tell yourself how beautiful you look today, what a great job you are doing at work. Compliment yourself for being a great friend, for taking tremendous care of your family or how wonderful it is that you are taking care of your body by eating healthy and exercising regularly.

You deserve a round of applause every day. Why not give it to yourself?

You yourself, as much as anybody in the entire Universe deserve your love and affection.

~ **Buddha**

Find Your Value and Worth

The only person in the world you can truly count on day in and day out is yourself. There are no conditions that must be met in order to accept and love yourself. You just have to give yourself permission to be open and to receive.

Break down those invisible barriers you build around yourself. Those barriers only create self-imposed limits and they are only causing you stress and pain.

How can you make yourself more open to receive? How can you ensure that those invisible walls stay down?

Action Step:

Reach out to 3-5 people you admire and love and ask them what your five best qualities are. Write them down in your journal.

Now compare what those people have said about you. Did they all say you had the same qualities? Are they all different? Are you surprised at what they said?

Being reminded of the great things about us can help us be more loving and gentle toward ourselves. Read this list every time you start to feel your self-worth or value wane.

The more you like yourself, the less you are like anyone else, which makes you unique.

~ **Walt Disney**

Put the Mask Away

There is no need to wear a mask or act fake just to please another. You are special all by yourself. You are extraordinary and you should never try to hide that.

Display your uniqueness for all to see.

Action Step:

I want you to become aware of when you are not being yourself.

Today, begin to take notice when you are putting on a mask. Who are you with? Where are you? What situation do you find yourself in? How are you acting? Now reflect your thoughts in your journal.

Do you feel comfortable being that person wearing that mask? If the answer is no, how can you change or what can you do differently when you find yourself in this predicament?

I'd rather be able to face myself in
the bathroom mirror than be
rich and famous.

~ **Ani DiFranco**

Become Your Own Best Friend

You can be rich and have all the money in the world and you can have fame where everyone you pass knows who you are, but if you don't like what you see every morning in the mirror, none of that will matter.

You can't truly enjoy your life, no matter what you have, until you can stand being in the same room with yourself.

Action Step:

Spend some quality time with yourself. Learn to become your own best friend. The fastest, most effective way to do this is to schedule ME dates.

A "Me Date" is when you take yourself out and participate in something enjoyable without having to rely on another to keep you company.

Take yourself out to a five-star dinner, take in that movie you are dying to see, go to that little coffee shop and enjoy a latte while reading a book, hike in the park while enjoying nature, or grab your bike and hit the trails.

It is irrelevant what you choose to do. The point is to get to know yourself, like you would your best friend. Love her. Talk to her.

To love oneself is the beginning of a
life-long romance.

~ **Oscar Wilde**

Fall in Love with YOU

What makes you—You? This is one of the questions I ask my clients all the time. The answers I receive never surprise me because I gave those same answers years ago when I was asked this very question. "I am ordinary…there is nothing special about me."

So not true!

You have so many qualities, both positive and negative that are amazing. Find them, love them, and be giddy over them. There is nothing better than having butterflies in your stomach over yourself.

Action Step:

Grab your journal and list all the qualities about yourself that excite you. Don't hold back…no one else has to see this list.

The next time your inner critic starts feeding you garbage about everything that is "wrong" with you, pull out this list and read it over and over again as a reminder of all your admirable qualities.

People who do not love themselves can adore others, because adoration is making someone else big and ourselves small. They can desire others, because desire comes out of a sense of inner incompleteness, which demands to be filled. But they can not love others, because love is an affirmation of the living, growing, being in all of us. If you don't have it, you can't give it.

~ **Andrew Matthews**

Create a Strong Relationship with Yourself First

Have you ever been dependent on someone else to make you feel complete or happy? Did that relationship last?

My guess is no because in order to really create a lasting bond of love between you and another, you must first love yourself.

What is one thing you can do now to strengthen your love for yourself?

Action Step:

Walk directly to your mirror; look deep into your eyes and say, "I love you. I appreciate you." This may be extremely difficult to do at first. It may feel like a big fat lie or seem excruciatingly embarrassing.

If you can't tell yourself I love you, then start with, "I am willing to believe that I can love you." Over time, I promise you, telling yourself I love you will feel and become more natural. Practice this every day.

Positive Thinking

Positive thinking is a mental attitude that allows you to anticipate happiness, joy, love, health and a successful outcome of every situation and action that you take. It is like having your own daily optimist sitting on your shoulder. I think it's high time you put your pessimist away.

I CAN is 100 times more important than IQ.

~ **Unknown**

Believe You Can Do It

You have the brain power to accomplish whatever you desire in life but if you don't believe it can be done, it will never happen.

Roadblocks will surface that will seem insurmountable, excuses will be given that seem completely realistic at the time but it is your job to ignore those excuses and crash through those roadblocks.

Action Step:

Grab your journal and write down one area in your life that you would like to change or improve. Is it your career? Perhaps your health? Your love life? Let's assume, you chose your love life. Now instead of listing all the things that are wrong with it and why it will never change, see if you can come up with ideas and ways you can improve it by shifting yourself.

For example, if you and your partner are having problems communicating, how can you personally help ease this issue? Could you change your tone of voice? Would asking him if now is a good time to chat work, rather than blurting out whatever it is you have to say? Should you learn to listen more and talk less? Take time to think about each others' feelings before jumping to the defensive?

Asking yourself how you can facilitate change is much more effective than creating excuses that get you nowhere.

There is only one way to happiness and that is to cease worrying about things which are beyond the power of our will.

~ **Epictetus**

Stop Being a Worry Wart

Always worrying about things we cannot control is a horrible way to live. Worrying about something does not make things happen faster or change a situation…only actions can.

Stop wasting your energy worrying, and instead spend that time thinking about what you can do to help in the situation. If you feel your circumstances are beyond your control, then let go of it and let things work themselves out on their own. Things truly happen if they are meant to happen.

This is by far the biggest lesson I have had to learn. Sometimes I still feel that I have miles to go.

Action Step:

Instead of just worrying about something important to you and letting it keep you up at night, list five actions that you could take immediately to change or enhance your situation. Of course, make sure these actions are within your control.

Fear less, hope more; Eat less, chew more; Whine less, breathe more; Talk less, say more; Love more, and all good things will be yours.

~ **Swedish Proverb**

Always Take Inspired Actions

Life is short. Make the most of the time you were given. Do not hold back. Always be and do more. Live by taking inspired actions. Because someday, you will be gone and you can never come back as the same person you were.

Aim for having no regrets. Live simply. Laugh often and love deeply.

Action Step:

What holds meaning to you? What really matters in your life? Is it your relationships? Your kids? Your career? Your passion? Every morning upon waking, I create the intention that I am going to participate only in things that bring more meaning to my life.

Creating this intention allows me to stop sweating the small stuff and to focus on what really, truly matters at the end of the day. I encourage you to do the same.

Before you go to sleep tonight, I want you to create your own intention. Write it down and post it on the bathroom mirror or on your closet door so it's one of the first things you'll see when you get out of bed.

The positive thinker sees the invisible,

feels the intangible,

and achieves the impossible.

~ **Unknown**

Envision Your Success

Not every goal is realized easily. When you find yourself feeling frustrated trying to reach a particular goal, picture what you can't see, imagine having your desire in your hand and then create the steps to make it happen.

Action Step:

Identify in your journal an important goal you have for your life. Envision the end result as though it has already happened. Next I want you to write down all the steps that you think were necessary to get you to the finish line. Just brainstorm. No need to worry about whether or not you forgot a step.

For example one of my long term goals was to write and publish a book but I had no idea how I was going to make that happen, nor did I have a clue where to start. Just thinking about it overwhelmed me. So I imagined holding the book in my hand first, and then I described, in as much detail as possible, what steps I took to reach the end result, in this case, a printed copy of my book. Sure, I missed steps but the point is, without making this list, I would have never started the book.

Now organize your steps into a logical order and start with the first one. As you move forward, everything will reveal itself.

Think like a queen. A queen is not afraid to fail. Failure is another stepping stone to greatness.

~ **Oprah Winfrey**

Do Not Play the Victim

I certainly have fallen on my face more times than I would like to count but the difference between me and someone who thinks that is a failure is I pick myself back up, dust myself off, and keep walking forward. I believe I have been this way since birth. I think it has something to do with being extra stubborn but I also believe it can be learned.

If you believe failure is not an option, then you can accept falling on your face is just the next step in your journey.

Action Step:

Grab your journal and reflect on a time when you felt like a failure. Can you look at the situation through a different lens? Can you view it as a stepping stone toward your success? Can you find one thing positive about that experience that can shift the way you feel about it?

I could have certainly played the victim with some of the experiences I endured in my life (rape, an eating disorder, financial mishap) but instead I used these circumstances to empower others.

What are you going to do with your circumstances?

When you get into a tight place and everything goes against you, till it seems as though you could not hold on a minute longer, never give up then, for that is just the place and time that the tide will turn.

~ Harriet Beecher Stowe

Persevere

I have been told many times when faced with adversity to hold on for just a little longer because it's often just when you decide to give up, that the result you were looking for is about to happen.

There is something to be said about those who never give up. I think they may be on to something.

Action Step:

When you are ready to throw in the towel, what are three things that you can do to stay in the game? Is there someone you can call to talk you through it? Do you schedule some ME time and come back to your project later? Do you sit down and re-evaluate your goals?

Whatever your action plan is going to be (steal mine above if you are stuck), write it down in your journal.

The next time you are ready to give up, open your journal and pull out this action plan. Use it. It works!

There are always flowers for those
who want to see them.

~ **Henri Matisse**

Look on the Bright Side

Is the glass half full or half empty? If you look at the glass half empty, you close the door to any new possibilities. If you view the glass as half full, you give yourself room to explore.

Which version would you like to live in?

Action Step:

Today, I want you to look at your life as if the glass is half full. How does that change the way you approach your life? How does that change the way you feel about yourself? Before you go to bed, write in your journal about your experience.

When you are in the valley, keep your goal firmly in view and you will get the renewed energy to continue the climb.

~ **Denis Waitley**

Keep Pushing Forward

Always imagine you see the light at the end of the tunnel. It will keep you motivated and determined to reach the end. It will inspire you to consistently take that next step.

Action Step:

Take one of your goals and imagine what it would feel like to see the light at the end of the tunnel. Describe that feeling in detail. How would it look? What would it allow you to experience?

If one of your goals is to be more fit, what would that look like to you? Would you have more energy? Feel sexier? Healthier? Would you be eating better? Exercising two times a week? Three times a week? Would your skin look brighter? Would your body feel stronger?

Associating a desired emotion to your actions has profound impact. It helps you press onward, and keeps you motivated because you want to have the desired outcome.

Worry often gives a small thing

a big shadow.

~ **Swedish Proverb**

Let the Little Things Go

Has there ever been something nagging you that you know you cannot change and have very little control over but you still let it eat away at you? Has that same little annoying thing ever stopped you from doing or achieving your dreams? Have you ever heard the saying "Don't sweat the small stuff?"

I know it is hard not to worry…I do it all the time but I also know that it can definitely get in your way.

Action Step:

Instead of worrying about that small thing you cannot change, learn to surrender. The little stressors do not have to be a big deal.

If you find yourself stuck in traffic, rather than go into road rage, why not put on some music and dance to the beat or belt out the words to the song? If you find yourself sitting in the doctor's office and you have been waiting a little too long for your appointment, rather than become irate with the receptionist, why not take advantage of the quiet time and practice deep breathing?

We have a choice how we react in situations that could potentially cause us stress. We can let it get us down or we can make the most of it. Which would you rather choose?

Stop focusing on the things you cannot change . . . put forth the energy in the things you can.

~ **Antonio Riggins**

Open the Door to the Possibility

Have you ever tried to change something you knew was an impossible feat? Or tried to force someone else to meet your expectations or standards?

Truth be told, there are so many things in your life that you have no control over. So why do you continue to spend so much of your time and energy playing a game you will never win?

I don't have the answer but I can empathize because I spent years trying to control everything that was out of my control. What I did learn is when I shifted my focus on to me, rather than everything else, my life changed. And a world of opportunity presented itself.

Action Step:

It is time to do some mind cleaning…to clear out the cobwebs in your brain that keep you stuck and keep you from focusing on what you actually have control over.

Today, I want you to write down everything you want to change in or about your life in your journal. Do not over think it. Just write whatever comes to your mind.

Now cross off all the things that do not hold meaning to you, that you have no control over, or that you no longer have passion around. Now look at what is left. Put your energy into those things.

Life/Attitude

Having a positive attitude helps you to cope more easily with the daily affairs of life. It brings optimism into your world, and makes it easier to avoid worry and negative thinking.

If you adopt a positive attitude as a way of life, it will bring constructive changes to your days that will make you feel happier, brighter and more successful.

With a positive attitude you see the bright side of life, become optimistic and expect the best to happen. It's a state of mind that is well worth developing and strengthening.

It is funny about life: if you refuse to accept anything but the very best you will very often get it.

~ **W. Somerset Maugham**

No Substitutions

You deserve the best. Accept no substitutions. If you believe that you should have something, the Universe will find a way to provide it.

Make no apologies for what you want.

Action Step:

Open your journal and list 20 of your deepest desires.

Do not worry about how they are going to happen or if they are going to come true. Just write them down. Declare to the Universe that this is what you want from your life.

Read these declarations aloud to yourself often. There is something to be said about declaring your desires to the Universe.

If you want things to be different,
perhaps the answer is to become
different yourself.

~ **Norman Vincent Peale**

Be the Change You Want to See

If you keep doing the same thing over and over again and always get the same result, then try something different. You may be surprised with the outcome. You may end up getting exactly what you always wanted.

Action Step:

If you are constantly trying to change someone else, alter the outcome of a specific situation or trying to control something that is out of your control, I want you to stop what you are doing right now.

Today, instead of doing what you always do, try something new. For example, if you are constantly nagging your boyfriend or husband to help you with the dishes, to take out the trash or to clean out the garage, chances are he is never going to do it. He probably, after the first time he heard you yelling or nagging about it, tuned you out.

Why not, instead, appreciate something he did do for you. Chances are, if you keep giving him positive feedback and cut out the nagging, those things you wished he would do miraculously happen.

Twenty years from now you will be more disappointed by the things you didn't do than by the ones you did do. So throw off the bowlines. Sail away from the safe harbor. Catch the trade winds in your sails. Explore. Dream. Discover.

~ **Mark Twain**

Nurture Your Dreams

It is great to have dreams but it is so much better to have those dreams turned into a reality. What if your dreams could come true? How would you look at your life differently?

Take action every day toward achieving your dreams. Live your life to the fullest. Stop hiding and start being who you were meant to be.

Action Step:

Create a vision board or a vision book.

Include words and pictures and whatever you can find that represents what your dream life would look like. Add statements to your vision board or book that imply you have already accomplished those dreams.

Look at your book often and keep adding to it. Share it with your friends, family and loved ones. Cultivating dreams are how they come true.

Attitude . . . is more important than the past . . . than circumstances, than failure, than successes, than what other people think or say or do . . . we have a choice everyday regarding the attitude we will embrace . . . We cannot change our past . . . we cannot change the fact that people will act in a certain way . . . The only thing we can do is play on the one string we have, and that is our attitude.

~ **Charles Swindoll**

Act As If

You get back what you put out in the world. If you want love, give love. If you want happiness, be happy.

A friend once told me "act as if" and eventually you won't need to be acting, you will just be what you desired.

Action Step:

What do you want out of life?

Do you wish to be a high powered corporate woman? Start by dressing like one. Do you wish to become a philanthropist? Start donating to your favorite charities now. Your $5 will eventually turn into $500 or more. Do you want to be an author? Start a blog.

Whatever it is you want out of life, don't wait for it to happen, take small steps to ensure you get there now.

Laugh as much as you breathe and love as long as you live.

~ **Unknown**

Keep It Simple

Don't take life or yourself too seriously. Have fun. Be light. Life doesn't always have to be filled with complications.

Life is what you make of it.

Action Step:

Every morning when we wake, we have a choice. We can make the most of our day and live it fully like it was our last or we can overcomplicate it, let our self-imposed pressure get out of hand and be downright miserable. Which version would you rather experience?

Today, I want you make every minute more enjoyable. When faced with something you would rather not do, ask yourself, "How can I make this more fun?"

For example, if you despise cleaning the house, why not throw some music on, and dance while dusting. Better yet, hire a cleaning service.

When you approach from this place of having more fun, two things happen. You actually have more fun and people are magnetically attracted to you. I call that a win-win.

Nobody can go back and start a new beginning, but anyone can start today and make a new ending.

~ **Maria Robinson**

Forget the Past

Stop living in the past. It is called the past for a reason…you cannot change what has already happened. Concentrate on the present and what you have to offer yourself and the world today.

You have the power to create anything you put your mind to. Don't let something you cannot change or take back, get in your way. Close the door to your past and open the door to the present.

Action Step:

Today, I want you to recognize your habit of either jumping into the future or trying to undo or correct the past.

Find a quiet space and sit down. Make sure both your feet are firmly on the ground. Breathe in and out for approximately 1-2 minutes, being mindful to what it going on with your body as you breathe.

For the next few minutes, notice any thoughts that you are having that involve the past or take you to the future. Acknowledge them, thank those thoughts and let them go.

If you get distracted, go back to your breathing and refocus. Notice how your mind moves in and out of the present moment. When you find yourself dwelling on the past or the future, bring yourself back to this visualization. Recall your thoughts, thank them and release them. Now you can enjoy the present moment.

To love is to risk not being loved in return. To hope is to risk pain. To try is to risk failure, but risk must be taken because the greatest hazard in life is to risk nothing.

~ **Unknown**

Take Risks

To be truly fulfilled, you must take risks. Without putting yourself out there, you will never truly be happy. Without taking a risk, there can never be a reward.

What kind of life would you have if you never took a gamble?

Action Step:

Today, start taking small risks. Push yourself out of your comfort zone.

For example, if you are terrified of public speaking, ask your friends or family to gather while you give a short 5-10 minute presentation. If you always wear baggy clothes to hide your body, perhaps wear a form fitting shirt or pants that actually fit. If you have been scared to tell someone how you feel about them, write it down and send it to them.

What one small risk are you going to take today?

If you let a mountain stand in the way of reaching your goals, maybe you need to ask yourself how badly you want it.

~ **Antonio Riggins**

Move Heaven and Earth

There is always a way around a roadblock. You might have to get creative but if you really want to accomplish something, you will find the way out.

I believe having determination and perseverance can hurdle any boundary life creates.

Action Step:

If you are faced with a goal you really want to accomplish, what are three ways you can ensure your goal is met?

Rather than waste your time thinking up all the reasons why you can't achieve your goal or why it will never happen, why not brainstorm some ideas of how you can make it happen?

For example, if you want to go to France but have no money or a way to get there, your list may include: get a loan, borrow the money, research exchange programs, look into house swapping, check to see if your frequent flyer miles will cover the flight, locate hostels and so on.

Now it's your turn. Grab your journal and start writing. Jot down all your ideas, regardless of how outlandish they may seem, of how you can make your goal happen.

Perhaps our eyes need to be washed by our tears once in a while, so that we can see Life with a clearer view again.

~ **Alex Tan**

Let It Flow

It is very important that we deal with our issues now, rather than shove them deep inside and let them fester for later. If you don't walk into the fire, I promise you will eventually get burned.

Holding on to negative emotions can drag you down, stop you in your tracks and make you feel immobile. Let it go. Scream at the top of your lungs, cry a river of tears but the point is to let it out and move on.

Action Step:

Be honest with yourself. What is one primary emotion you have been feeling lately? Are you angry? Sad? Resentful? Has this emotion been stewing inside you for days, weeks or months?

It is time to release it! This emotion is not serving you.

What are some ways that you could let this emotion go? Would screaming help? Crying? Calling a friend? Writing about it and then tearing it up or burning it? Do you need to throw something? Grab some boxing gloves and a punching bag? What about a long run? A yoga class?

Try one of these ideas or try them all. Just do something.

Happiness depends upon ourselves.

~ **Aristotle**

Don't Worry, Be Happy

You have the power to be happy. It is a conscious decision that only you can make. Once you can accept that others do not determine your happiness, I promise, you will start to think differently about your life.

What makes you happy? What puts a smile on your face? Lights you up? Fills your heart?

Action Step:

Grab your journal and start brainstorming and identifying all the little things that make you happy.

Is it feeding the birds in your backyard? Is it hearing your child laugh? Smelling fresh cut flowers? Walking into your bedroom and seeing the bed made? Seeing no dishes in the sink when you come home from work? Playing with your dogs? Cats? Spending some time in nature? Taking a bubble bath? What about a steaming hot shower with essential oils? Is it cuddling at night with your man on the couch before you go to sleep? Savoring a glass of red wine or a piece of dark chocolate?

Whatever is on your list, do these things regularly. Not just once in awhile. Make time for them every day.

Acceptance

Self acceptance is being happy with who you are. It is a pact with yourself to appreciate, validate, accept and support who you are right now—even those parts you hate and would eventually like to change.

Acceptance of what has happened is the first step to overcoming the consequences of any misfortune.

~ **William James**

Lesson Learned

Have you ever felt like it was impossible to move on after something terrible happened to you? It is completely understandable. It can affect all your decisions and actions moving forward. It can also stop you dead in your tracks.

I know fear sets in. I have been there. What helped me was to accept that it happened, acknowledge it was a lesson learned and plow forward knowing something great was ahead.

Action Step:

Grab your journal and write down three difficult experiences or losses you faced in your lifetime. Next to each experience, reflect on what lesson you learned from it and what you gained from the experience.

Have these experiences made you wiser? Smarter? Has it enhanced your life in any way?

Human beings, like plants, grow in the soil of acceptance, not in the atmosphere of rejection.

~ **John Powell**

Nurture Yourself

If you neglect a plant, it will die. You need to water it, feed it, talk to it and it will thrive.

The same goes for humans. If you neglect yourself, you probably won't die but you will suffer…you will feel unloved, hungry for attention and alone. In order to make sure you thrive, you must nurture yourself every day.

Action Step:

In your journal, create a list of 10 things that you could do for yourself today that will make you feel loved and cherished. These ideas must help you thrive. This should not be a list of things you think you "should" do.

Does your list include eating healthy food? Taking that 20 minute walk in the park? Scheduling some much needed time off from work? Soaking in a warm bath? Reading your favorite novel? Meditating?

After you create this list, schedule one of them each day for the next 10 days. Then, rinse and repeat. Keep it going. This should become a regular part of your routine.

If you accept the expectations of others, especially negative ones, then you never will change the outcome.

~ **Michael Jordan**

Do Not Be a Follower

Leaders are not followers. Make the decision to be a leader. Do not accept others' expectations if they are not in line with your own.

Dare to be better. Dare to be different.

Do you find yourself following others? Are your thoughts and values in line with your beliefs? If you find yourself adapting to meet someone else's expectations and it doesn't feel right, have the courage to change your direction.

Action Step:

Today, I want you to tune in to what is going on in your world. I want you to approach every situation with the courage and the conviction to ask for what you desire.

It can be as simple as telling your partner what you want for dinner or what movie you would like to go see rather than your usual comment of "I don't care, whatever you want is fine."

Speak up. Let people know what you crave. Ask for things you feel you deserve. Be the leader in your own life.

Instead of always comparing yourself to others . . . find a mirror and come to terms with what you see.

~ **Kimberly Riggins**

No More Comparing

Have you ever looked at someone and wished you had her lips, her eyes or her hair? I would bet that same person you wish you looked liked, wishes she looked like someone else too.

The important thing to remember here is if you are wishing for something that is impossible to achieve, you will always find yourself deeply disappointed.

Instead it would be in your best interest to accept what you were given and learn to love those attributes.

Action Step:

In order to stop comparing yourself to everyone else, you must first practice seeing others as potential allies, rather than rivalries.

Choose one person you compare yourself to and instead of falling victim to comparison, get to know her. Learn about her interests, passions, ideals. How can she become a friend rather than an enemy?

Write down your experience in your journal.

Whether it is the best of times or the
worst of times, it is the only
time we have.

~ **Art Buckwald**

Make the Most of Every Day

There will be days that you wish never happened and days that you wish would never end.

You should embrace them all. Make the most of whatever your day throws at you because someday, your time will come.

You never want regrets…just the memories of being the best you could be and savoring every moment.

Action Step:

Celebrate yourself and all the little things that happen to you daily. You should acknowledge and reward yourself every day.

Why not make yourself a special dinner and use the good china? Break out the bubbly and have a glass of champagne rather than wait for New Year's Eve. Wear that special dress just because. Pull out that lingerie and wear it to bed, rather than saving it for your one time a year vacation.

Moments are meant to be cherished regardless of how big or small. Start celebrating you and your life today.

.

Be who you are and say what you feel, because those who mind don't matter and those who matter don't mind.

~ **Dr. Seuss**

Acknowledge Your Feelings

Loving yourself requires you to be truthful about your own feelings. If you are happy, acknowledge the joy. If you are sad, acknowledge the sorrow. If you are angry, acknowledge the anger.

When you are truthful about your feelings, you will be set free. You will no longer need to censor yourself to please someone else, nor will you have to stuff your feelings and pretend to be someone you are not. How refreshing!

Action Step:

What emotion do you always try to hide?

Today, I want you to allow yourself to feel what you are feeling. Don't stuff it, feed it, quiet it or ignore it. Let it consume you.

If you are angry, scream with rage, grab some boxing gloves and punch the bag, put on your sneakers and go for a sprint, call a friend and ask them if you can vent.

How did it make you feel to let it out? Write your thoughts down in your journal.

Consult not your fears but your hopes and your dreams. Think not about your frustrations, but about your unfulfilled potential. Concern yourself not with what you tried and failed in, but with what it is still possible for you to do.

~ Pope John XXIII

Don't Give Up

We all have dreams and desires. It is what we do to achieve them that matters. Focus on all the possibilities life still has in store for you because if you don't, you will always find yourself stuck, facing a barrier you cannot cross.

Action Step:

Create a bucket list. Be as outrageous or as simple as you want to be. The sky is the limit. List everything you ever dreamed of doing.

Do you want to take a cruise to Santorini, Greece? Learn how to play the guitar? Write your first book? Eat gelato in Italy with a dark, handsome stranger? Stand in front of the Eiffel Tower at sunset? Skydive? Have a romantic picnic in a hot air balloon? Skinny dip in the ocean? Make wild passionate love on the beach? Eat a lavish breakfast in bed?

Now start crossing things off your list. Make them happen now. Get creative. Do not wait until you are old and gray and can barely walk. Your dreams and desires deserve to be fulfilled today.

The way I see it, if you want the rainbow, you gotta put up with the rain.

~ **Dolly Parton**

Kiss a Frog . . . Find Your Prince

My father always said what doesn't kill you makes you stronger. You have to endure conflict to find resolution.

I know that it isn't easy but I promise it will have all been worth it.

As the fairy tale goes, the princess had to kiss the frog to find her prince. Like the princess, you might have to do something that may be uncomfortable and do it over and over again until you find what you're searching for.

Action Step:

Do something uncomfortable today. Test your boundaries and play on the edge.

If you've desired to spice up your sex life, why not take the initiative yourself, rather than wait for your man to take the reigns? Why not put on some lingerie if you never wear it? Walk around the house naked? Cook dinner in your panties? Flirt like you did when you first met?

If you're single and would like to meet a man, why not go on that blind date? Join a dating service? Go on a singles retreat?

Test yourself. Creep toward the edge of uncomfortable. Get your blood rushing. There is nothing more exciting than the unknown.

Understanding is the first step to acceptance, and only with acceptance can there be recovery.

~ **Joanne Kathleen Rowling**

Look Within

When I was suffering from anorexia, I thought I would never be "whole" again. I believed I was a lost cause. Rather than face myself, I consistently made excuses for my behavior and I blamed everyone else for my issues.

It wasn't until I hit rock bottom and stepped back and away from my disorder that I realized the only person I was truly hurting was myself.

When you are down and out and feeling lost, turn and look within. What looks like a mess now could end up being a tremendous gift. If it wasn't for that period in my life, I wouldn't be doing what I am today.

Action Step:

Grab your journal and recall a negative experience in your life. What good can you take away from it? There is always a silver lining to our black clouds.

The minute you settle for less than you deserve, you get even less than you settled for.

~ **Maureen Dowd**

Never Settle

You have the power to attain anything you want in life. Don't lower your expectations out of fear that you can't have it all. It doesn't make you selfish or conceited that you think you deserve the best.

Always ask for more than you want. Never settle.

Action Step:

Decide here and now what you want out of your life. If there were no obstacles, what would you want to achieve? Have? Do? Be specific.

If you want to be wealthy, how much money would you like to have? If you want to own a vacation home, where would it be? What would it look like? How often would you visit?

If you want to meet the man of your dreams, what would he look like, what kind of personality would he have? How would the two of you communicate?

If you wish to sail around the world, where would you go? What ports would you stop at? Who would you meet on your journey? Would you invite others to join you?

Now it's your turn. Grab your journal and write. Your life is waiting.

About the Author

Kimberly Riggins is a dynamic, outspoken, health and wellness coach who is the founder and creator of The Art of Eating Chocolate Naked. Her mission is to help all women, including you, learn to nourish their bellies, love their bodies and accept themselves. She is also determined to eradicate negative self-talk everywhere and of course, to accomplish this with a small side of kick-ass fun.

In fact, she is 100% committed to you and all women who are tired of determining their happiness with the way they look. Life doesn't have to be about your shape or size. Life shouldn't be about sacrifices...it should encompass fun, passion, acceptance, happiness and lots of sexy indulgences. Kimberly teaches you through some unconventional ways how you can get there.

Her ideas may be a little outside of the box but she has tried them all and is a true believer in their success. As a teenager, Kimberly was a body-hating, insecure girl who ended up suffering from anorexia. Today she is a body-confident, sassy, sensual woman who embraces her flaws and uses them to her advantage.

Her credentials speak for themselves. She is a Board Certified Holistic Health and Wellness Counselor and Coach, accredited with the American Association of Drugless Practitioners (AADP). She holds a Bachelor of Science in Psychology, a Master of Science in Holistic Nutrition and has been certified as a Personal Trainer and Fitness Instructor.

She is a coauthor of the book, "The Gratitude Project: Celebrating 365 Days of Gratitude," and founded and facilitates The Love Your Naked Ass Warrior Series, monthly teleclasses that feature inspiring female luminaries who are defying the social norm in unconventional ways. She is currently brainstorming new ideas for her next book involving sensuality.

When she is not trying to change the world's views on beauty and body image, she is relaxing at home in Pennsylvania indulging in her two favorite foods, dark chocolate and wine, with her family and their Yorkshire terriers, Zoe and Fritz.

Learn more about Kimberly at www.KimberlyRiggins.com.

Get Your FREE Copy
of the Teleclass

"Stand Naked: How to Truly Love Yourself from the Inside Out without Having to Change a Thing about Your Body"

Listen to this recording to discover:

💜 The top 3 mistakes women make when they are trying to feel better about themselves.

💜 How to change your negative self-talk by retraining your brain.

💜 Why befriending your inner critical bitch is so important.

💜 The #1 thing that you can do instantly that will help you feel sexier and more beautiful in your own skin.

💜 How forgiving yourself for not having the perfect body can actually open up the door to new possibilities.

💜 Six more ways you can love your body.

💜 And much more…

Get your FREE copy of this teleclass at:

www.KimberlyRiggins.com/stand-naked

Grab Your Copy of the Mirror Mantra & Body Love Kit

If you want to learn how you can ooze sexual confidence that will have men dropping at your feet and women wondering what your secret is, then you need to grab your FREE copy of The Mirror Mantra & Body Love Kit today!

To get this audio download and PDF workbook, go to:

www.KimberlyRiggins.com/free-gifts

Notes